PREPARE AND PAINT YOUR BACKGROUND

French country painting often shared the fresh colours of Breton rustic pottery. Primrose yellow, shades of French blue, and touches of white give the floral motifs a springlike charm.

Preparation can be minimal. Make sure surfaces are clean and non-greasy. Gloss finishes – paint or varnish – need sanding back with medium-grade sandpaper to provide a 'key' for the paint. No need to fill cracks and surface blemishes; these add character to a rustic painted piece. The kitchen cabinet and table shown here were both painted with standard matt emulsion paints. Emulsion is the modern decorator's choice because it dries fast, is easy to apply, and provides an excellent surface for decoration. In this case, it also imitates the 'lean' texture of eighteenth-century painted furniture, the result of using paints with a very low linseed oil content.

TO GIVE EXTRA DEPTH OF COLOUR
TO PLAINLY PAINTED SURFACES,
THE TECHNIQUE USED OVERLAYS TWO
SHADES OF YELLOW MATT EMULSION,
THE BRIGHTER COLOUR ON TOP. THE
BRIGHT TOP COAT IS RUBBED BACK
WITH MEDIUM-GRADE WET-AND-DRY
PAPER JUST BEFORE IT DRIES.
WET-AND-DRY PAPER, WHICH IS FINER
THAN SANDPAPER, IS NOT ESSENTIAL,
BUT AVOIDS THE RISK OF RUBBING
THROUGH BOTH COATS.

TWO SHADES OF BLUE EMULSION
HAVE BEEN USED HERE IN THE
SAME WAY. NOTICE HOW THE
STRONGER COLOUR EMPHASISES
THE GUTSY TEXTURE AND GRAINING
OF OLD WOODEN SURFACES.

A POSY OF COLOUR

The clear blues and yellows of our French-inspired kitchen corner are set off by a rich green background colour. Sophisticated rustic is the mood of traditional French painted decoration, and it is amazing what this artless style does for the unrelated assortment of pieces shown here – some of them antique, some plain junk – bringing them together harmoniously as part of an overall effect. Not all the pieces are wood. Toleware, or painted metal, is distinctively French and two examples are shown: a spoon rack and a delightful antique petrol can. On the rush-seated sofa motifs have been used sparingly, but these underline its attractive shape and character. The table is a very utilitarian kitchen piece with an enamelled top, transformed here with primrose paint and a blue flower spray. Note how carrying out a single colour theme 'ties' objects together.

PAINTING WITH A PATTERN

Painting simple little sprays will build up your confidence.

Shown here are the steps involved in tracing off and painting the simple pair of motifs we arranged to enhance the cut-out top of the wooden rail.

Points to remember: ● Use a hard lead pencil for the tracing down because this will give you a clear outline. ● Keep a clean copy of the tracing patterns – you might like to photocopy them a few times. You can then cut them up to fit awkward spaces without worrying about losing the originals. ● If you cut smaller pieces of transfer paper, be careful to leave yourself a big enough piece for the largest motif. ● Most of the patterns in this book were painted with fast-drying artist's acrylic colours, available in tubes from all artist's suppliers. These dry with a matt finish, and are used thinned with a little water to 'single cream' consistency. Use an old plate as a palette. ● Use soft watercolour brushes in different sizes to paint motifs, including one fine one for outlining. There is no need to buy expensive sable brushes – synthetic bristles or mixed hair are fine.

TRACING DOWN AND FILLING IN

Symmetrical patterns are easy to do and always look at home in this style of rustic decoration.

1 FIX PATTERN IN PLACE WITH MASKING TAPE. SLIP TRANSFER PAPER BENEATH. TRACE PATTERNS CAREFULLY AND FIRMLY WITH SHARP PENCIL.

2 USE CENTRAL FLOWER TO LINE UP SECOND HALF OF SYMMETRICAL FLOWER SPRAY. (TURN TRACING OVER.)

3 USING MEDIUM BRUSH, FILL IN PATTERN SHAPES (EXCEPT STEMS) WITH COLOUR A.

4 WITH FINER BRUSH, USE COLOUR B TO PAINT IN OUTLINE USE VERY LIGHT PRESSURE WHEN PAINTING FINE STEMS OR LEAFY TENDRILS.

MATERIALS CHECKLIST

WELL-SHARPENED HARD LEAD PENCIL, SCISSORS, MASKING TAPE, OLD PLATE, WATER JAR, KITCHEN PAPER OR TISSUES FOR WIPING BRUSHES, RULER OR TAPE FOR POSITIONING MOTIFS.

ACRYLIC COLOURS IN WHITE, RAW UMBER, COBALT AND ULTRAMARINE BLUE.

TWO WATERCOLOUR BRUSHES, ONE FINE, ONE MEDIUM.

COLOUR RECIPES:
(A) WHITE WITH TOUCH OF RAW UMBER
(B) ULTRAMARINE WITH TOUCH OF RAW UMBER

5 BALANCED ARRANGEMENTS ARE USED ON COUNTRY FURNITURE FOR HIGHLIGHTING DECORATIVE SHAPES: CHAIRBACKS, BEDHEADS, THE CORNICE OF A DRESSER OR CUPBOARD, FOR EXAMPLE. THERE IS AN ALMOST CALLIGRAPHIC QUALITY TO THESE STROKES. PRACTICE WILL ENABLE YOU TO ACHIEVE THE SAME EFFECT, AND TO EXECUTE EACH STROKE IN ONE SWEEP OF THE BRUSH.

PAINTERLY TRICKS OF THE TRAD

The decoration on small objects that are handled and looked at closely needs to be more controlled and subtle. Here we show some ideas for you to copy in order to add quality to your painting.

1 THERE IS NO NEED TO KEEP REPEATING THE SAME SIMPLE BORDER TRACING. CUTTING A CARD TEMPLATE LIKE THE ONE HERE, AND USING IT TO PENCIL AROUND AN OBJECT, MAKES THE JOB MUCH QUICKER. INDIVIDUAL BRUSH STROKES WILL GIVE THIS DESIGN MUCH MORE VIVACITY THAN IF IT WERE CAREFULLY AND EVENLY FILLED IN.

3 FORM 'LEAF' SHAPES NATURALLY AND EASILY WITH A SOFT WATERCOLOUR BRUSH. APPLY BRUSH TO SURFACE, PRESS AND GENTLY RELEASE OUT OF STROKE. 'COMMA' SHAPES FOR PETALS ARE FORMED BY APPLYING GREATER PRESSURE INITIALLY BEFORE TAPERING OUT.

4 THE 'DRY BRUSH' TECHNIQUE IS USED TO GIVE TEXTURE AND FORM TO ROSE PETALS. BLOT MOST OF COLOUR OFF ON KITCHEN PAPER, AND TEST BRUSH ON SHEET OF PAPER FIRST. THERE SHOULD BE JUST ENOUGH COLOUR ON THE BRUSH TO LEAVE A CLOUDY LINE.

AUTHOR'S TIP

It really is worth practising making brush strokes like the ones shown here on spare sheets of paper before launching on a piece as attractive as this. The whole expressiveness of this type of decoration lies in the spontaneity and variety of the brush strokes.

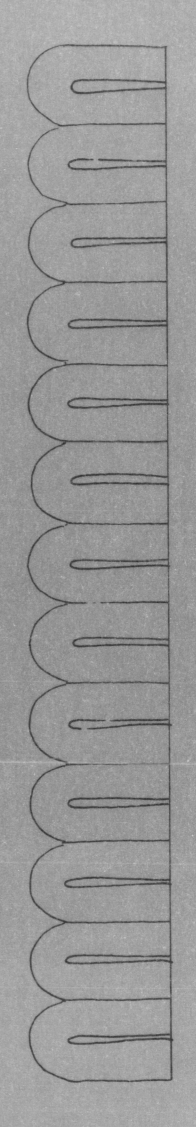

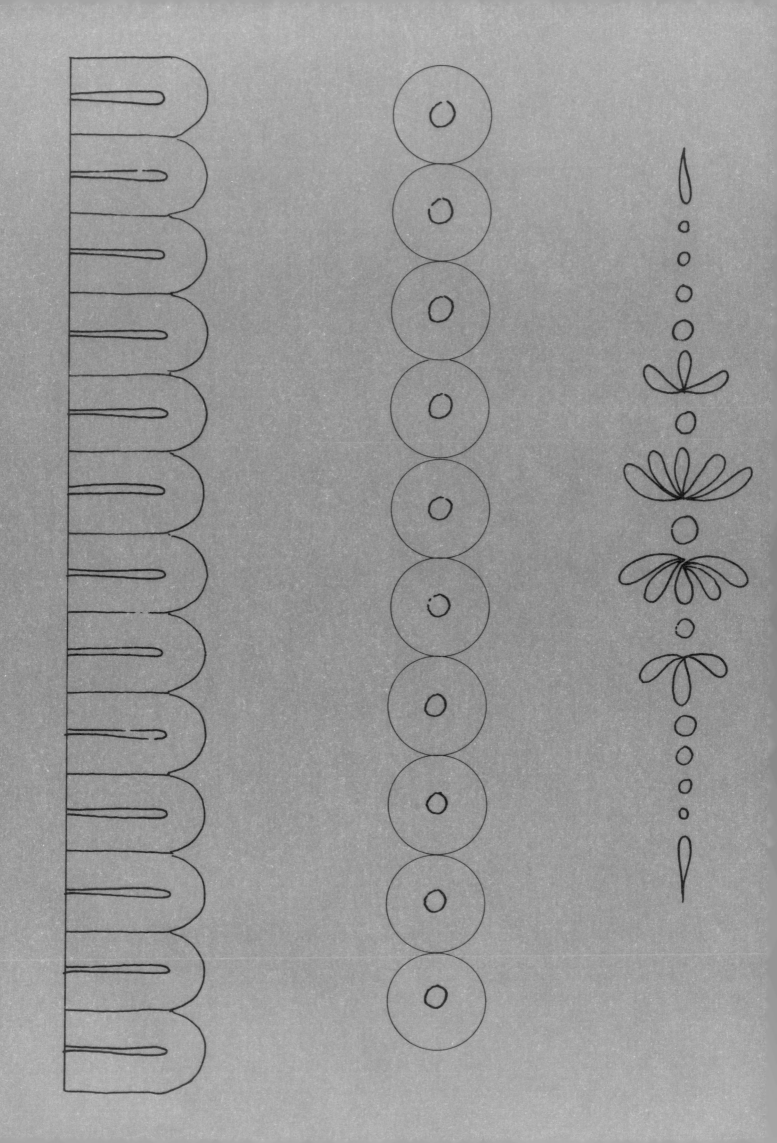

●

THIS PAPER PROTECTS
THE BLUE TRACING PAPER

●

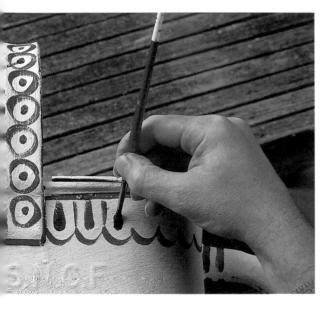

2 MAKE YOUR BRUSH WORK FOR YOU. THE CHARM OF THIS VERY BASIC BORDER MOTIF COMES FROM THE LOOSE AND IMPRESSIONISTIC USE OF BRUSH STROKES TO 'DASH' IN THE SHAPES.

5 THE COMPLETED PETROL CAN SHOWS THIS SORT OF DECORATIVE PAINTING AT ITS SPIRITED BEST: PRACTICE IS NEEDED TO PERFECT LOOSENESS IN BRUSH TECHNIQUE.

COLOUR RECIPE

ONE COLOUR USED FOR ALL STAGES: ULTRAMARINE BLUE WITH TOUCH OF RAW UMBER

ACRYLIC MEDIUM, ALSO CALLED PVA, CAN BE MIXED WITH ANY ACRYLIC COLOUR FOR THINNER PAINT AND HENCE GREATER FLOW.

1 USING COLOUR A, BRUSH IN ALL MAIN OUTLINES, STEMS AND LEAVES.

4 COLOUR C IS USED TO HIGHLIGHT LEAF SHAPES AND TO ADD DOTS.

COLOUR RECIPES

(A) ULTRAMARINE WITH TOUCH OF RAW UMBER

(B) 2 PARTS COBALT BLUE, ONE PART WHITE, TOUCH OF RAW UMBER

(C) WHITE WITH TOUCH OF ULTRAMARINE BLUE

By now you are beginning to feel relaxed and confident with your brushwork. A different approach is being used here for the main flower piece in our French painting patterns. All the main outlines are brushed in first with blue, as expressively possible.

2 FILL IN PETALS AND SOME LEAF SHAPES USING COLOUR B TOWARDS OUTSIDE AND COLOUR C TOWARDS MIDDLE.

3 PAIRS OF LEAVES ARE DRAWN OFF CENTRAL STEM IN COLOUR A. HERE, BRUSH STROKES BEGIN FINE, THEN ROUND OUT TO CREATE LEAVES.

5 SMALL PENDANT DESIGN IS BRUSHED IN DOWN TABLE LEG USING COLOUR A.

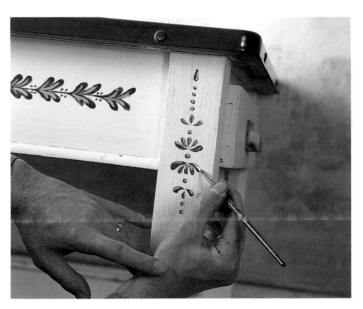

6 THESE SHAPES ARE HIGHLIGHTED AND SOFTENED WITH COLOUR B.

AUTHOR'S TIPS The painting hand often needs support when working in the middle of a surface. Usually, resting it on your free hand provides a steadying base. As it is invariably easier to paint designs on a horizontal surface, on tricky shapes try turning the piece, and tip furniture on its side as necessary. Also, most painting of this sort has a 'direction', so always orient yourself appropriately.

FITTING
FLOWERS

Play around with your pattern elements before deciding which looks best where.

Flower sprays and borders are ideal for long narrow spaces, like the side of this table, or the little drop ornament on the leg. The narrow formal border makes a feature of the attractive shape of the rush-seated sofa. You need to spend more time on the planning than on the actual painting in many cases.

THE LARGE FLORAL MOTIF, CARRIED OUT IN FULL COLOUR ON THE ENAMEL TABLE TOP, ALMOST HAS THE LOOK OF HAND-PAINTED PORCELAIN. THE PAINTS USED ARE TRANSPARENT GLASS PAINTS, OBTAINABLE FROM SPECIALIST TRADE SHOPS. THESE PAINTS ARE ALMOST AS HARD AS ENAMEL SO ON A SURFACE LIKE THIS A VARNISH IS NOT NECESSARY. THE PAINTABILITY TRANSFER PAPER DOES NOT GIVE CLEAR IMPRESSIONS ON A SHINY SURFACE LIKE THIS: HERE WE SUBSTITUTED ORDINARY CARBON PAPER.

THE SAME MOTIF INTERPRETED IN THE SAME COLOURS, YET ON A DIFFERENT BACKGROUND COLOUR AND ARRANGED DIFFERENTLY, CAN PRODUCE A SURPRISINGLY DISTINCTIVE RESULT. THE 'PAIR OF LEAVES' BORDER IS USED ON THE FRAME OF THE SOFA AND THE SIDE OF THE TABLE. ON THE SOFA, CURVING IT SLIGHTLY AND TAPERING IT OFF TOWARDS THE BOTTOM GIVES IT A MUCH MORE DELICATE EFFECT.

It takes very little time to decorate small items like the quartet on this page, but the results can be charming.

CLEVER RE-JUGGLING OF THE BASIC PATTERN MOTIFS HAS MADE A DELIGHTFUL OBJECT OF AN ANTIQUE FRENCH PETROL CAN. THE BORDERS EMPHASISE THE SHAPE OF THE CAN VERY ATTRACTIVELY. NOTE THE LIVELY BRUSH STROKES WHICH GIVE THE FLOWER SPRAY SO MUCH CHARACTER. ACRYLIC PAINTS OVER AN EMULSION BASE WERE USED HERE.

THIS LITTLE CABINET WITH ITS BEVELLED PORTHOLE MIRROR IS AN IDEAL PIECE TO PAINT, SO DECORATIVE IN ITSELF THAT IT ONLY NEEDED A LITTLE HELP FROM OUR PAINTING PATTERNS.

THE SAME FLOWER SPRAY AS ON THE SPOON RACK, SLIGHTLY ADJUSTED, IS PAINTED WITH ACRYLIC COLOURS ON A FLAT EMULSION BASE. THIS IS ACTUALLY AN AUTHENTIC FRENCH MAILBOX, LOOKING PRETTY ENOUGH TO BE PROMOTED TO THE KITCHEN.

THE UTILITARIAN CHARACTER OF AN ENAMEL SPOON RACK HAS
BEEN COMPLETELY DISGUISED BY THE FRENCH FLOWER SPRAY,
CARRIED OUT IN TWO SHADES OF BLUE ONLY. USING GLASS
PAINTS AGAIN HAS GIVEN A WATERCOLOUR-LIKE TRANSPARENCY
TO THE STANDARD MOTIF.